AMAZING SCIENCE

PIRANHAS

AND OTHER

WONDERS OF THE JUNGLE

Q.L. PEARCE
Illustrated by Mary Ann Fraser

Julian Messner

To Zachary Maxwell, the boy who loves books   *—Q.L. Pearce*
To my mother for all her support   *—Mary Ann Fraser*

Acknowledgments

With thanks to Mycol Doyle, Ph.D., Rancho Santa Ana Botanic Gardens, Claremont, California, for his invaluable assistance and critical review of the manuscript. Thanks also to Lisa Melton of RGA Publishing for asking all the right questions.

Library of Congress Cataloging-in-Publication Data
Pearce, Q. L. (Querida Lee)
   Amazing science. Piranhas and other wonders of the jungle / Q.L. Pearce ;
illustrated by Mary Ann Fraser.
     p. cm.
   Includes bibliographical references.
   Summary: Surveys the exotic species of plants and animals that
live in the world's rain forests.
   1. Rain forest fauna—Juvenile literature. 2. Rain forest
ecology—Juvenile literature. [1. Rain forest ecology,
2. Ecology.]   I. Fraser, Mary Ann, ill. II. Title. III. Title:
Piranhas and other wonders of the jungle.
QL112.P4 1990   90-6022
574.909'3—dc20   CIP

Contents

Jungles and Rain Forests

Tropical rain forests, popularly called jungles, can best be described by one word: variety. There is a greater variety of life in the rain forest than in any other environment on Earth. One square mile of these rainy regions may contain 300 kinds of trees. One hundred types of plants and vines may live among the branches of a single tree. Certain rain forests are home to not hundreds, but many *thousands* of animal species, most of them insects.

The tropical rain forest is made up of several different levels, or layers, of life. In the uppermost **emergent layer,** the crowns of huge trees branch out in the sunlight. Although not the tallest trees in the world, these giants may reach 200 feet or more in height and can live to be 800 to 1,400 years old.

Fifty feet or so beneath the top of the emergent layer is the **canopy,** an unbroken, leafy-green carpet in the air that stretches for miles. The canopy is a sunlit, treetop world filled with colorful birds, buzzing insects, and in some areas, troops of chattering monkeys. Little sunlight penetrates to the **understory** below. This level, which is between 35 and 80 feet from the ground, is made up of trees that can survive in low light as well as young trees waiting for a chance to reach the canopy.

Although most people picture the **jungle floor** as a tangle of trees and plants, it's actually open and easy to walk through. However, it is a damp, dark place. Usually the humidity (the amount of water vapor in the air) is about 95 percent. That means the air is holding just about as much water vapor as it possibly can. Less than two percent of the sunlight that strikes the canopy filters through to the forest floor.

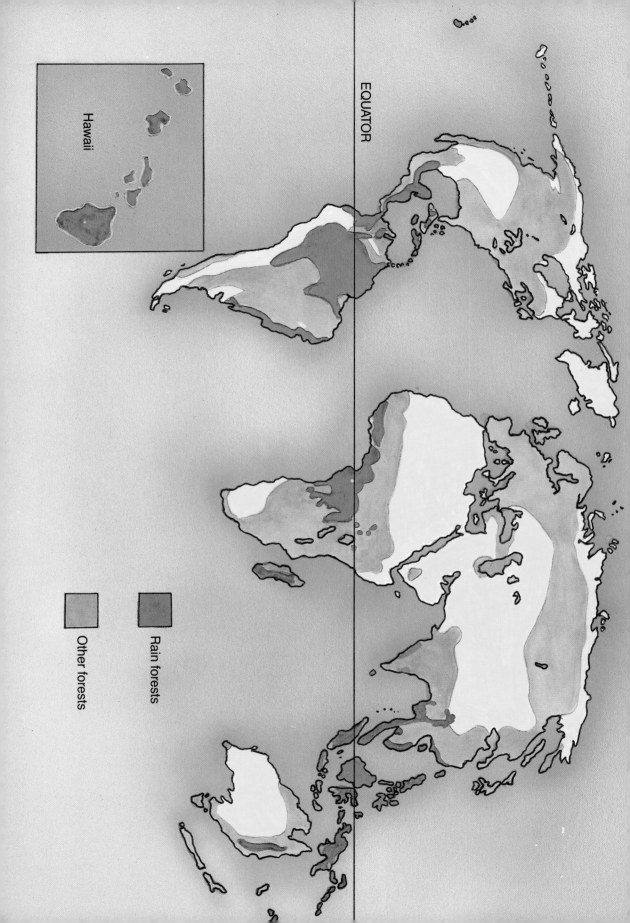

EQUATOR

Hawaii

Other forests

Rain forests

The Equator

If you were to look at a map of the world, you'd see that the earth's tropical rain forests roughly straddle the equator. Within this area are the very special conditions needed to form a tropical rain forest—a warm, constant temperature, steady rainfall, and plenty of sunlight.

At the equator, the sun is nearly overhead throughout the year. During the long days, its rays strike the earth almost directly and warm the area evenly. To the north and south of the tropical zone, the temperature from winter to summer can change as much as 100°F. But at the equator, it varies little more than 10°. Here, the temperature difference between winter and summer is usually less than the difference between day and night.

Three-quarters of the area within the tropical zone is covered by ocean water that is constantly evaporating. Water vapor is carried upward on warm, rising air. When this air meets the cool air above it, the water vapor condenses and falls as rain. Since near the equator water is always evaporating, rising, and condensing, the average rainfall in the tropics is about 150 inches per year. (The average annual rainfall in Los Angeles is only about 15 inches.) The world's wettest rain forests are in Hawaii. Some places on the islands of Kauai (cow-EYE) and Maui are drenched by more than 450 inches of rain per year!

Rain forests differ in altitude, distance from the equator, and amount of rainfall. Tropical or equatorial rain forests develop in sheltered, well-drained lowlands. Little or no seasonal changes occur there and rain falls throughout the year. Montane forests (forests in the mountains) occur in rainy highlands where the temperature can change dramatically between day and night.

Other forests, called monsoon forests, have a dry season, but enough rain falls during the wet season to allow us to consider them rain forests.

Rain forests, indicated by dark green, thrive in the tropical zone that lies along the equator.

The Amazon Jungle

Did you know that over one-third of the world's jungles are within the borders of a single country? The huge Amazon rain forest, which is mainly within the borders of Brazil, covers an area nearly the size of Australia. Flowing through the heart of this great jungle is the Amazon River, which is second in length only to the Nile River of Africa. Although not the longest, the Amazon is surely the mightiest of rivers. During maximum flood period, it carries to the Atlantic Ocean one-fifth of all river water on Earth.

The vast jungle that surrounds the river contains nearly 80,000 different plant species. Many valuable plants and trees originated in this South American jungle, such as the peanut and pineapple plants, and the rubber tree and cocoa tree. There are hundreds of unique jumping, creeping, and flying animal species, too. Unlike monkeys in Africa and Asia, many monkeys of the Amazon, such as the spider monkey, have prehensile (or grasping) tails that can be used to wrap around and grasp tree branches. The canopy is filled with chattering birds and thousands of brilliantly colored butterflies, such as the magnificent, giant blue morpho.

Besides the powerful, stealthy cat called the jaguar and the three-foot-high, hoglike tapir, there are few large mammals in the Amazon. It is home, however, to the world's largest rodent—the capybara. This four-foot-long relative of the guinea pig may weigh in at more than 100 pounds. Here, too, one of the world's largest spiders, the bird-eating spider, roves the leaf litter of the jungle floor. With a body about three and a half inches long and a leg span of 10 inches, this Frisbee-sized spider occasionally snares and eats small birds.

An immense variety of plant and animal life can be found in the huge, lush Amazon rain forest.

The Jungles of Africa

Dozens of adventure novels and films have been set in the jungles of Africa. These tales give readers the idea that the African rain forests are impenetrable green webs of plants and vines. Such jungle really can be found along sunny riverbanks, but the "shadowy" interior is actually fairly open. The forests begin on the West African coast near the equator and follow the course of the Zaire River. The climate becomes drier in East Africa and the tropical forest gives way to huge grasslands. Some animals commonly thought of as jungle beasts, such as the lion, actually live on the grasslands.

The jungles of Africa are home to many incredible creatures. During the day, gorillas, the largest of the primates (or apelike creatures), browse peacefully on fruit and leaves. Found here, too, are many "little" giants. The giant snail is eight inches long and weighs as much as a small hamster. At five and a half inches long, the goliath beetle, one of the world's largest insects, is about the length of your hand. The beautiful giant swallowtail is a butterfly with a wingspan as wide as this page is long. Hidden on the darkened jungle floor lurk snakes and other reptiles, including the five-and-a-half-foot-long Gabon viper. This reptile holds enough venom to kill 20 people! Its fangs, which can be up to two inches in length, are longer than those of any other snake in the world.

The trees of the African jungle are not as varied as those of other tropical rain forests, but they are as remarkable. You may be surprised to know that a mid-sized African tree called *Cola nitida* (NIT-ih-duh) is the source of the flavor and caffeine in cola drinks. Natives sometimes chew the reddish seeds of this tree's star-shaped fruit for extra energy.

The dense African jungles are home to the chimpanzee, okapi, and hundreds of different reptiles, birds, and insects.

Australasian Jungles

The trees and plants of Australasia (or "southern Asia") live according to a special rhythm. These jungles are part of a monsoon rain forest with distinct wet and dry seasons (see page 57 for a description of monsoons). This rain forest stretches across the Asian peninsula, crowds onto the islands of Indonesia and the Philippines, and traces a slim line along the northern coast of Australia.

Because of the several-months-long dry season, many of the plants that make up the Australasian jungle have developed ways to conserve water. Some go into a resting state during this time. Trees such as the lofty 150-foot-tall teak shed their leaves and do not sprout new ones until the rains come again. Other remarkable plants include an Asian relative of the violet. In most flower gardens, violets grow only a few inches tall, but in the Australasian jungles they may reach 80 feet tall. Woody grasses called bamboo tower 120 feet high, and some grow as much as 16 inches per day! Along the muddy island shores, roots of mangrove trees loop out into the salty water. To escape predators, small fish called mudskippers leave their watery home and climb up on the mangrove roots or skip along the shore.

The Australasian jungles blanket thousands of islands. Some animals are unique to a single island. Java is a large island roughly the size of Florida. The forest at its western tip is the home of one of the world's rarest large mammals, the Javan rhino. At one time this animal roamed much of Indonesia. Now only about fifty animals are left. About 11 feet long and weighing more than a ton, the Javan rhino spends its time browsing in the dense forest or wallowing in a muddy stream or shallow lake.

The rare Javan rhino shares its home with other unusual creatures and plants of the Australasian rain forest.

Garcinia punctata tree

bark shavings used to
treat diarrhea

Wild yam

root used to
relieve pain

Nasturtium

flowers used to treat
scurvy and bronchitis

Cinchona

bark used to produce
quinine, which treats
malaria

Nature's Medicine Cabinet

What do a jungle and a modern hospital have in common? One in four medicines used daily in hospitals has its origins in rain forest plants. Jungle plants have, in fact, been used for centuries to heal everything from stomachaches to skin rashes. Relatives of these plants may even grow in your own garden. The nasturtium (nuh-STER-shum) is a delicate little flower with seeds that are a powerful laxative and petals that are an excellent source of vitamin C. The flowers are also used to treat scurvy and bronchitis. The wild yam, a member of the lily family, has roots that produce a substance used to relieve pain. (This twining plant is also an important food source in many jungles throughout the world.)

Many of the healing plants are more exotic. The bark of the cinchona (sin-KO-nuh) tree, or fever tree, of South America is the source of quinine (KWY-nine). Although synthetic drugs are now more practical than quinine, this substance was the only treatment for malaria for centuries. Curare (kyoo-RAHR-ee) is a tarlike paste made from jungle vines. A deadly poison, curare was used by Indians, who dipped their arrow tips into the paste. Luckily, it has probably saved many more human lives than it has taken. Scientists discovered that a small amount of turbocurarine, a substance that comes from curare, is helpful in treating such human diseases as multiple sclerosis.

In the earth's rain forests, there are probably hundreds of useful plants that remain undiscovered. Perhaps the key to future medical treatments is at this moment growing in a shadowy corner of a jungle floor. Careless destruction of the rain forest with its many unusual plants may be more costly than we think.

Rain forest plants have been used for centuries to treat illnesses of all kinds.

Cloud Forest

Can you imagine an icy-cold glacier within sight of a warm, tropical rain forest? If you were standing on one of the peaks in the Ruwenzori Mountains of Uganda, you'd see this amazing sight. Six of the peaks in this African mountain range tower more than two miles high and are capped by immense rivers of ice, or glaciers. The forest that clings to the mountain slopes belongs to one of the world's strangest types of jungle—the cloud forest. The name *Ruwenzori* means "rainmaker," and it is well deserved. Wrapped in mist, the forest receives up to 200 inches of rainfall per year. Shaggy moss in shades of deep green, golden yellow, and red carpets the ground and drapes trees and vines. Even the remains of fallen trees are laced with moss. During the day, plants and animals bake in the equatorial heat. When evening falls, however, the jungle becomes cold and wintry. In fact, it is not unusual for hail to fall.

In this extraordinary place, plants can grow to an amazing size. For instance, wild heather, which grows only about two feet tall in other areas, can reach higher than a two-story building in the Ruwenzori Mountains. A garden lobelia normally has small blossoms. A lobelia of the Ruwenzoris blooms with flower spikes as tall as a grown man. This special plant has also developed a way to survive the frosty nights. The lobelias have shiny, silvery leaves that close at night. The temperature within the tightly wrapped leaves may be several degrees warmer than the outside temperature.

Because of the misty climate of the Ruwenzori Mountains, plants like wild heather and lobelias grow to amazing heights.

The Jungle Canopy

Did you know that many jungle animals spend all of their lives in the treetops? The trees provide all the leaves, fruit, nuts, and seeds the animals need to eat as well as a dense, leafy shelter. Insects, brightly colored birds, and dozens of other animal species live and die in the lofty jungle canopy.

Ninety feet or more above the ground, the three-toed sloth of South America clings to branches, using its strong, curved claws. Because of the constant humidity, algae often grow on this creature's damp fur, tinting it green! This animal is so adapted to life in the trees that it is practically helpless on the ground. Its muscles are too weak to support its own weight, so on the ground the three-toed sloth can only crawl.

The sloth shares its treetop home with the amazing howler monkey, the largest monkey of the Amazon rain forest. However, it isn't its size that distinguishes this creature, but its eerie cry. A large hollow bone at the base of the animal's tongue acts as a sort of amplifier. The ear-splitting wail of the howler monkey can be heard for miles.

Some of the loveliest and sweetest-smelling jungle flowers can also be found high in the canopy. The flowers' colorful blossoms attract insects and hummingbirds that pollinate the flowers. Tropical fruits, such as the fig, invite parrots, macaws, yellow-eared bats, porcupines, and other animals to a luscious meal. Hundreds of tiny creatures live in the treetops, too. Treefrogs, water beetles, and snails live in tree-dwelling plants called bromeliads (broh-MEE-lee-adz). Water captured in the center of the bromeliads makes a comfortable home for these creatures.

The sunlit jungle canopy is home to an incredible variety of fruits, flowers, insects, birds, monkeys, and other plants and animals.

Magnified slime molds

7x

1.5x

Slime Molds of the Jungle Floor

Imagine a sticky, slimy wave that creeps slowly forward, flowing over or around every living thing in its path. No, it's not a creature from science fiction, it's a slime mold of the jungle. This unusual life-form has characteristics of both plantlike fungi and animals. The slime mold begins as a slippery mass on the dark underside of rotting logs or in damp soil. It moves slowly, feeding on bacteria by flowing around and then absorbing them. When temperature and moisture conditions are right, the slime mold oozes toward the surface of the log or soil to reach the light. There, the small gooey blobs develop into flowerlike bodies of re-markable color and shape. They may be red, yellow, or purple. They may be cottony puffs, hairlike strands, or mats of tiny, shining beads. Some are so small that they can be seen clearly only through a microscope.

The purpose of these flowering bodies is to produce and release spores. Spread by rain, wind, or passing ani-mals, each spore contains a living cell that will form a new slime mold. The single cell behaves much like an ordinary single-celled creature. In fact, many of these cells develop flagella, which are hairlike structures common to single-celled creatures. The flagella act as tiny propellers, moving the slime-mold spores from place to place across a moist surface.

The scientific name for slime molds, *Myxomycetes* (miks-o-MY-set-eez), is a combination of the Greek words for "slime" and "mushroom." Still, some scientists prefer the term *Mycetozoa* (my-see-toh-ZO-uh), or "mushroom animals."

Plant or animal? The amazing slime molds of the jungle floor behave like both!

A Tree Falls

The jungle is always changing and rearranging. Violent storm winds can rip huge holes in the canopy. Landslides can clear riverbanks and topple even the tallest, strongest trees. When a giant tree comes crashing down, it can take many smaller trees with it, forming a gap or clearing. Generally, trees that make up the canopy layer produce seeds, but many never sprout. The few that do sprout must fight to survive, competing with other plants for nutrients in the poor soil.

When a tree falls, suddenly opening a clearing and allowing sunlight to reach the jungle floor, an incredible race begins. The fallen tree begins to decay, releasing nutrients into the soil. Joining it are many small, shade-loving trees and plants, which die in the hot sun. With plenty of nutrients, sunlight, and water, the seedlings that have been waiting for the right conditions soar upward. The first to make the move are known as pioneer trees. They can stand the strong sun and sudden changes in humidity and temperature. The balsa of South America, a tree valued for its tough, light wood, is a well-known pioneer tree.

As dozens of seedlings take root and dash for a place in the sunlit canopy, small trees that had been trapped in the dark understory bolt upward as well. For decades these trees lived in the shadow of the giants, their branches held in close to their trunks. In a burst of growth, these trees reach the canopy in only a few years. There, they spread their branches, exposing thick leafy crowns. The winners have earned a place in the sun. Within fifty years, the space in the canopy is filled. The trees below, now blocked from the nourishing sunlight, must wait for another opportunity.

When a tree falls, it knocks down everything in its path and clears the way for a small patch of sunlight to enter the rain forest.

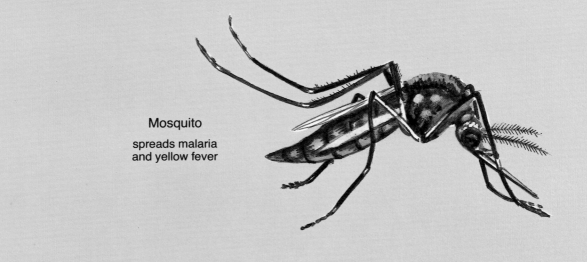

Mosquito

spreads malaria
and yellow fever

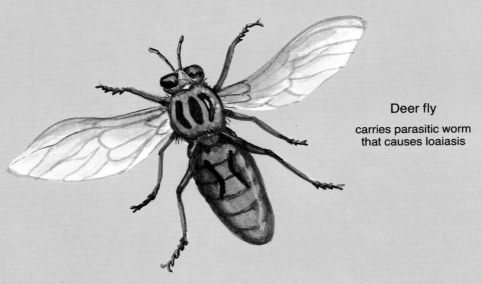

Deer fly

carries parasitic worm
that causes loaiasis

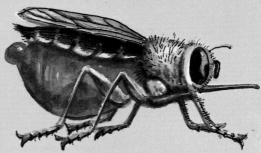

Tsetse fly

carries organisms
that cause
sleeping sickness

Disease Carriers

About a thousand years ago, a creature no larger than a housefly halted an army. Islamic soldiers were invading Central Africa when their horses and camels began to die by the hundreds. The enemy that stopped the advance was the tsetse fly. Today, this insect is responsible for the death of thousands of people each year in Africa. The tsetse feeds on blood. While it feeds, microscopic deadly organisms pass from the insect to its victim. These organisms cause a disease in humans called sleeping sickness.

The tsetse fly does not begin its life carrying these terrible organisms. Rather, when it first bites an infected person or animal, the fly picks up and then carries the organisms to their next target. Sleeping sickness begins with fever and swelling in the neck. The sufferer becomes very tired and sleeps a great deal. Without medical treatment, victims of sleeping sickness never wake up again.

Although smaller than the tsetse fly, the anopheles (uh-NAHF-uh-leez) mosquito is more dangerous. Found in tropical areas all over the world, this insect has been responsible for the loss of millions of lives to one of humankind's most dreaded diseases—malaria. The male anopheles mosquito dines harmlessly on the nectar of flowers. But the female needs a meal of blood to provide protein for her eggs. She pierces the skin of humans with her long, slender mouthpart. She then pumps in saliva, which keeps the blood from clotting. Disease-causing organisms enter the victim through this saliva. Before long, the first symptoms—soreness and backache—appear in the victim. These are followed by chills, fever, terrible thirst, drenching sweats, and, without proper medical treatment, death.

With only a tiny bite, the mosquito, deer fly, and tsetse fly transmit deadly diseases.

Liana-vine
holding devices

Lianas and Strangling Vines

Best known as Tarzan's method of transportation, lianas are woody jungle vines. Some are slender, but others may be up to two feet wide and more than 300 feet long. Lianas need to reach the sunlit canopy to survive, but they don't have to do it alone. They are hitchhikers, clinging to host trees by hooks, tendrils, and light roots that burrow into the trees' trunks. Some species grow steadily higher up the host, while others simply hang on to young saplings and are drawn upward as the supporting trees grow. When they finally reach the canopy, the lianas weave a tight web. In giant, snakelike coils, the vines twist and loop from branch to branch and tree to tree, filling every available opening to light. They mesh so tightly, in fact, that they make it difficult to cut down jungle trees. Even when a tree is cut through, the tangle of vines above may hold the tree in place. Lianas and other jungle vines can be useful, though, and you could probably find one or two products from vines in your own home. Raffia, a vine palm, is the source of rattan, used to make light, durable baskets and furniture.

Another kind of vine, the strangler fig, is not the harmless tenant that lianas are. Beginning life as an air plant tucked safely in the forked branch of a host tree, the strangler fig soon develops slim roots that grow toward the ground. Once rooted in soil, the fig vine draws in nutrients and grows quickly. As the roots thicken, they surround the helpless host inside. The strangler fig robs the host of nutrients from the soil. It blocks the host tree's leaves from the sun with its own leaves. The host dies and soon rots away. By that time, the strangler fig's roots are strong enough to support the weight of this completely hollow "tree."

Lianas and strangling figs—nature's hitchhikers—reach the jungle canopy by clinging to host trees in a number of ways.

Giant Water Lilies

Although it's called a lily, the giant water lily is not a lily at all. Rather, it's a member of an ancient group of freshwater plants that first developed around the time of the dinosaurs. Also known as the royal water lily, this plant is the largest of its kind. Its huge, saucer-shaped leaves, or pads, can grow to seven feet in diameter. This water lily lives in slow-moving backwaters of the Amazon River. Firmly rooted in the mud, the plant sends thick, fleshy stems toward the surface of the water. These stems are covered with short, sharp spines that discourage hungry fish and insects from making a meal of the plant. Ridges on the underside of the pads form raised patterns that trap tiny air bubbles on the leaf surface between the ridges. Because of this, the jumbo leaves float easily in the water.

Some stems support cuplike flowers that have as many as 50 petals and that spread up to 18 inches wide. The cream-colored blossoms open at night and release a strong, perfumy scent. This attracts beetles and other insects that pollinate the plant. After that happens, the giant water lily produces small, leathery berries containing seeds. When the berries release them, the seeds float away or simply sink and take root near the parent.

Giant water lilies provide food and shelter for countless creatures. Insects and fish feed on the seeds and deposit their eggs on or under the impressive pads. Local Indians grind the high-protein seeds into flour. A bird called the jacana (juh-KAHN-uh) is particularly well suited for strolling across the floating vegetation. Its long, slender toes spread more than five inches wide. This distributes the six-ounce bird's weight over a large area, allowing the jacana to balance easily on the pad while it hunts for insects on the waxy surface.

The giant water lily provides food and shelter for countless creatures, among them the tiny jacana.

Echolocation

Vampire Bats

Have you heard the tale of the vampire Dracula? A fictional evil count from Transylvania, Dracula sucked the blood of living victims and often took the form of a bat. Count Dracula is only a storybook character, but his namesake, the vampire bat, is a real creature, and well named, too: It's the only mammal that feeds solely on blood. There are three kinds of vampire bats and they roost in hollow trees and darkened caves throughout Central and South America. They're not as big as you might have imagined: The largest is less than four inches long and has a wingspan of about one foot.

The vampire bat survives on the blood of such animals as cattle, pigs, dogs—and, sometimes, humans. A nocturnal creature, it flies through the dark night searching for prey. This bat uses echolocation to detect a meal, which is a lot like the radar used on planes. The flying bat emits a series of high-pitched sounds. The sound waves bounce off anything in their path. From the strength of the echo and the time it takes to return, the bat knows where an object is and if it is food. Once it has located a meal, the bat lands on the ground near its prey and scurries into position. Then, with its sharp front teeth, it scrapes a patch of the animal's skin until it begins to bleed. The vampire bat doesn't suck the blood but laps it up as it flows from the wound. Although one bat rarely takes enough blood to harm the victim, it's not unusual for several bats to feed at once on the same creature. Still, blood loss is not the greatest danger of this bat's bite, but rather the diseases it may carry, such as rabies.

In spite of its unpleasant eating habits, the vampire bat is very gentle with its own kind. These animals carefully groom each other's soft fur. The young are cared for particularly well. Female vampire bats help each other to raise their babies and will even adopt a needy orphan.

Central and South American vampire bats: the only mammals that feed solely on blood.

Humans in the Jungle

Looking down on a vast green jungle from an airplane, you might think that the rain forest is deserted. From that height, there are few signs of human life. But people do live in the world's rain forests. In fact, in the Amazon, anthropologists have discovered that humans have lived there for at least 10,000 years. When the Europeans arrived in the 16th century, about 5 million Indians lived in the Amazon basin. Today, there are far fewer Indians, but the river is as important to them as it was to their ancestors.

To the Indians, the Amazon River has always been a source of food and transportation. Homes are thus built near the water. Since the river level rises once a year, the homes are built on stilts. People who live on the flood-plain have adapted to the rise and fall of the water in other ways, too. When the river is low, they plant crops that grow quickly, such as corn and rice. These can be harvested before the floodwaters return.

The African rain forest is the land of the Mbuti (mm-BOO-tee) people, also called the pygmies. Known for being small, the pygmies average about four and a half feet tall. They are friendly people who refer to their jungle as "father" or "mother." It provides them with food, clothing, and shelter. The Mbuti live in small groups of 20 to 100. They build their homes from branches that are bent to form a domed frame, then covered with leaves. The durable homes can be built in less than an hour. There are no chiefs in the Mbuti villages, and no prisons either. When a person commits a crime, he or she is shamed. No one will look at the wrongdoer until a certain amount of time passes. The person is then forgiven for the misdeed and allowed to rejoin the group.

The dense African rain forest provides the Mbuti people, also known as pygmies, with everything they need to survive.

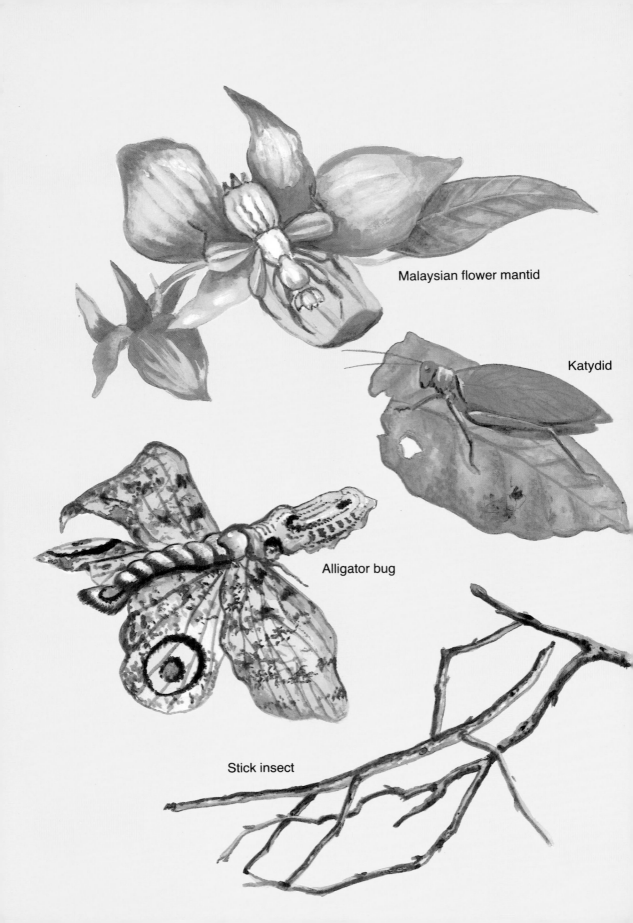

Malaysian flower mantid

Katydid

Alligator bug

Stick insect

Masters of Disguise

Scientists have identified hundreds of thousands of kinds of insects in the rain forests. That may sound like an amazing variety, but thousands more may exist, still waiting to be discovered. With so many of these creatures in the jungle, the competition for food is fierce. One interesting tactic insects use to obtain food is disguise. Many use camouflage to blend in with their surroundings and, in so doing, trap unwary prey. Others use disguise to avoid becoming the main course themselves! Triangular-shaped treehoppers that gather together along a branch look very much like thorns. Stick insects resemble dry twigs. These "twigs" can be from one inch to one foot long. Perhaps the most unusual masquerade is that of the alligator bug. Its tactic is not to blend in with its background but to confuse its enemies by looking more like a reptile than an insect. Its shape and pattern make it look like a tiny alligator head, complete with a toothy smile.

Behavior can also be an important part of the charade. Some insects remain perfectly still for long periods of time and go unnoticed by predators. Others, such as the katydid, use movement as a part of their disguise. The katydid looks like a dry leaf. Clinging to a branch, it sways slightly as if it were being blown by the breeze.

Mantids are also masters of disguise. Green, leaflike mantids prowl in the trees and shrubs for flying insects. Thin, brown, twiglike mantids hunt in the leaf litter for grasshoppers and beetles. The camouflage of the Malaysian flower mantid serves a double purpose. It looks so much like a pink orchid when it remains still that it can safely "hide" in plain sight. The mantid's predators think it is a flower and are uninterested. Its prey also mistake it for a flower, but the prey fly in close for a meal of nectar, only to be trapped by the hungry flower mantid.

These insects have developed amazing, and successful, disguise tactics to fool their hungry predators.

The World's Largest Primates

If you wanted to imitate a gorilla, what would you do? Perhaps you'd beat your chest and roar, trying to look fierce. It's true that a male may try to frighten a stranger by beating his chest, stamping on the ground, and ripping up vegetation. But that is only a small part of gorilla behavior. Gorillas are not dangerous creatures unless they are surprised or wounded. Left in peace, they are gentle animals that spend their days searching for leaves, stems, and fruit to eat. Some even seem to have a taste for red ants.

Like humans, gorillas are primates, a group of animals that includes monkeys and apes (such as the orangutan and chimpanzee). Although only four to six feet tall, they are the largest of our relatives. A male can tip the scales at more than 550 pounds, which is up to three times the weight of a human male of the same height. Although a gorilla's outstretched arms may reach eight feet from hand to hand, the animal is not built for swinging in trees. Rather, gorillas live in small family groups on the ground. At night, they sleep in nests made of leaves and branches. Females and their young sometimes build their nests in the trees, but the hefty males usually settle on the ground below.

Gorillas dwell in the jungles of Africa, and, if undisturbed, they may live to a ripe old age of 35 years or more. Only two kinds are known to exist, and sadly, both are endangered. In the west, brown-furred lowland gorillas live in the forests of Camaroon, Gabon, and Zaire. Eastern gorillas ramble in the montane rain forests of Uganda and Rwanda (ruh-WAN-duh). These animals have come to be called, simply, mountain gorillas. Thick black fur covers their bodies. When males reach 10 or 12 years of age, a large patch of fur on their backs turns a silvery color. Now adults, the males are nicknamed "silverbacks."

Despite their fearful appearance, gorillas are actually gentle creatures and strike out only in self-defense.

The Aye-Aye

The tiny, nocturnal aye-aye (EYE-EYE) has an undeserved reputation. According to the native legends of Madagascar, a huge island off the southeastern coast of Africa, one touch from this animal causes death. Although the legend is untrue, in the past, humans have killed this shy little creature out of fear. Because of that and because humans are changing the natural environment of Madagascar, the aye-aye is now seriously in danger of becoming extinct.

When the aye-aye was first discovered, scientists thought it might be a rodent related to such animals as rabbits and squirrels. Actually, on the tree of animal life, the aye-aye shares a branch with its fellow primates, the apes, monkeys, and humans. The confusion was due to the aye-aye's odd teeth. Its front teeth are long and curved like those of a rodent, and they continue to grow throughout the animal's life. The aye-aye uses its teeth to gnaw into wood, which also wears the teeth down and keeps them from growing too long.

At night, the tiny one-and-a-half-foot-long, five-pound aye-aye hops from branch to branch in the understory, searching for insects and insect larvae to eat. With its excellent senses of hearing and smell, the aye-aye can detect insects burrowing deep in the wood. When it has discovered a possible meal, it gnaws quickly into the branch, then pries out its dinner with its uncommonly long and slender third finger. The aye-aye also enjoys fruit, particularly coconut. Chewing a hole in a coconut husk is no problem for this creature, and its slim finger is perfect for scraping out the juicy meat.

The aye-aye may look like a strange sort of rabbit or squirrel, but it's actually related to monkeys, apes, and humans.

Winged Royalty

If there is a ruler of the upper levels of the Amazon rain forest, it is probably the harpy eagle. This bird, the mightiest of eagles the world over, has little to fear from other creatures. It patrols high in the canopy and emergent layers of the rain forest spying for prey. With its powerful legs—stronger than those of any other bird of prey—the harpy eagle can easily pry a struggling capuchin monkey or three-toed sloth from a branch. The feet of this feathered powerhouse are the size of a man's hand and are designed to grip with crushing force. Each toe is tipped with a sharp, inwardly curved claw to hold on to prey. The eagle's short, broad wings allow it to dive into the leafy canopy with tremendous agility and speed.

The harpy eagle may rocket through the treetops at speeds of up to 50 miles per hour, and it is agile enough to capture another bird on the wing. Still, the harpy eagle often hunts in short flights from tree to tree. Since its hearing is as excellent as its eyesight, this eagle often locates prey by perching quietly and listening for the prey to move among the leaves.

The female harpy eagle is slightly larger than the male. She is about three feet long and weighs up to 20 pounds. Every other year, both female and male build a flattened nest of twigs and branches at least 150 feet above the jungle floor. Here they raise usually two eaglets. Together, the parents feed meat to the young birds after first carefully removing the prey's fur. As the eaglets grow older, they begin to imitate the killing of prey: When their parents bring them food, although the prey is already quite dead, the eaglets "kill" it several times before devouring their meal.

Ruler of the Amazon jungle canopy, the harpy eagle can soar up to 50 miles per hour in its hunt for prey.

Colorful Canopy Birds

Some of the world's most beautiful birds inhabit the canopies of tropical rain forests. These splendid creatures are of an incredible variety. They range in size from the three-foot-long hyacinthine macaw of Brazil to the three-inch-long pygmy parrot of New Guinea. Among the most magnificent of jungle birds is the rare quetzal (ket-SAHL) of Guatemala. The bird is strikingly feathered in emerald green with trailing, three-foot-long tailfeathers and a brilliant red breast. An Indian legend says that the colors of the quetzal did not always include red. According to the legend, in 1524, a Mayan chieftan was killed by the Spaniards. A quetzal settled on the dying man's chest. When the mournful bird flew away, its breast was forever stained the deep red of blood.

It's not colorful feathers that draw attention to the toucan of South America, but its spectacular bill. The nearly one-foot-long, hollow bill is serrated along the edge and painted with streaks of yellow, blue, green, or red. With its bill, the bird plucks fruit from nearby branches. Tossing the fruit into the air, the toucan opens its bill wide and lets the morsel drop in. When sleeping, the toucan lays its beak across its back and covers it with its wings and tail.

Jungle trees the world over are filled with hundreds of chattering, vividly colored parrots in every shade of the rainbow. These birds use their powerful curved beaks for crunching hard-shelled nuts and seeds, and to steady themselves as they climb among the branches. Sadly, because of their beauty, parrots are often captured and sold as pets. Many of them do not survive shipment, and those that do are fated to live out their lives in cages far from their natural home.

The toucan's huge, elaborately striped beak adds a
splash of color to the tropical rain forest.

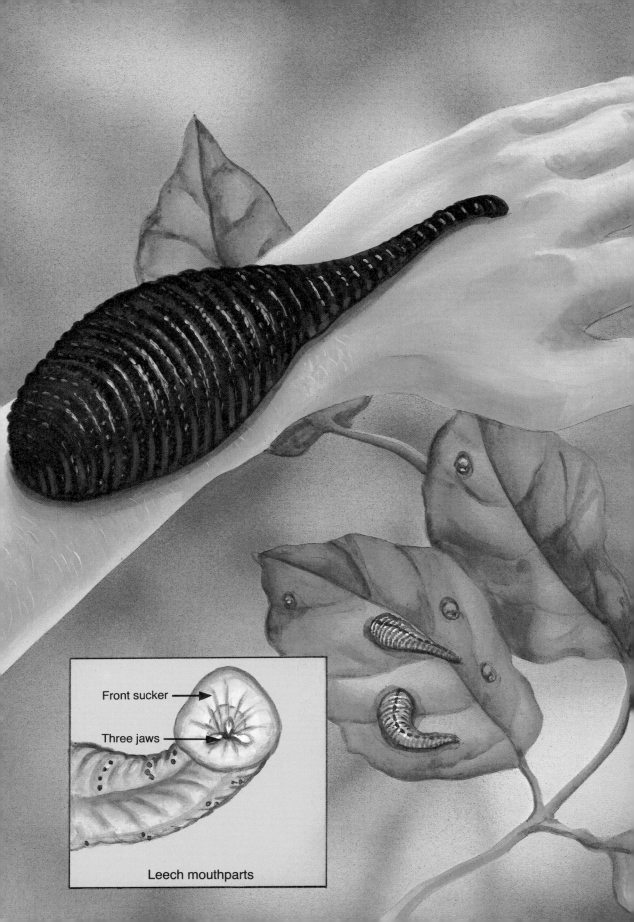

Front sucker

Three jaws

Leech mouthparts

Creepy Leeches

A trek through damp jungle growth brings explorers in contact with some of the world's most unpleasant hitch-hikers—leeches. Members of a large group of animals called annelids (AN-uh-lidz), leeches are related to earth-worms. Some leeches feed on snails or worms. Other leeches feed on the blood of fish and other animals, including humans. Certain African and Asian leeches enter an animal's nose or throat and attach themselves to the soft membranes inside, clogging the air passages. The host often dies, not from blood loss, but from suffocation. On a human, the leech clings to bare skin. Victims often claim that they cannot feel the bite of a leech. As the dis-agreeable creature bites, it seems that it may transfer a sub-stance that deadens the pain of the wound. The leech also releases chemicals that cause the victim's blood vessels to relax, which keeps the blood flowing freely. Scientists are studying these substances to help them develop treat-ments for certain blood disorders.

To help it move, the leech has suckers at each end of its body. On land, it inches along by bracing the front sucker and pulling the rear end of the body forward, then bracing the rear sucker and pushing the front end forward. In water, the leech moves by flattening its body and flutter-ing up and down. The leech can swim upside down and even "tread water" while searching for prey, such as fish.

The giant Amazon leech, as its name suggests, is the largest leech in the world. A full 18 inches long, or about the length of a house cat (not including the tail), this creature feeds on the blood of its prey through piercing mouthparts that may be up to six inches long. It may not surprise you that this freshwater leech can consume 5 to 10 times its own weight in blood in just 30 minutes.

An enormous blood-sucker, the giant Amazon leech attaches itself to humans or animals for nourishment.

The Water Boa

The anaconda of the Amazon region is the world's heaviest snake. Some people claim the anaconda is the longest snake, too, although the Asian python is also a contender for the title. The largest confirmed size of an anaconda is 275 pounds and 30 feet long—that's longer than two cars parked bumper to bumper. Even newborn anacondas are impressive. A female can give birth to more than three dozen live young, each nearly a yard long!

An excellent swimmer, this huge reptile, nicknamed the water boa, stays near water. The anaconda may drape itself along a heavy branch overhanging a river or stretch out on a sandy bank, but it often lingers in the shallows at the water's edge. The anaconda's nostrils are at the top of its snout so it can lie almost completely hidden under water while waiting for a meal. It preys on fish and water-dwelling reptiles, and on mammals and birds that come to drink. This powerful animal does not generally attack humans, but it will defend itself if threatened. Although not venomous, the anaconda is certainly deadly. It kills by constriction. First, it wraps its muscular body around its prey. Then, with each exhalation of the victim, the snake tightens its coils. The captured animal is unable to take in a new breath and suffocates within a minute or two. The anaconda doesn't chew its food but swallows it whole. After a big meal, it may stretch out for several days to digest it.

The first snakes that developed millions of years ago were also constrictors. They probably evolved from burrowing lizards. The giant anaconda has two tiny spurs on the underside of its body that are all that remain of the hind legs of the creature's lizard ancestors.

One of the world's largest snakes, the anaconda, a constrictor, can make an easy meal out of the capybara.

The Matamata

In certain areas of the Amazon basin, to call someone "cara de matamata" or "face of a matamata" is considered a terrible insult. The appearance of this 8-to-16-inch-long, swamp-dwelling turtle is certainly bizarre. Its triangular-shaped head is flattened and its wide mouth turns up at the edges in a sort of silly smile. It has tiny eyes and a long, snorkel-like snout. Unlike most turtles, the matamata cannot draw its head into its protective shell. When threatened, it bends its long snakelike neck into an S-shape and tucks its head safely under the overhanging ridge of its shell.

The matamata may look strange to us, but its appearance serves as perfect camouflage. Its ridged, bumpy shell makes it look like a pile of rotted wood or leaf litter. During the day, this small reptile hides among the real leaf litter or digs itself into the dark mud on the banks of stagnant ponds or sluggish streams. At night, it shuffles into the dim, murky water to hunt. There, too, it is well camouflaged. Algae actually grow on the matamata's shell. Although the matamata can hunt actively, it doesn't really need to; it can lie quietly under water and wait for its prey to come to it. It can hold its breath for up to forty minutes or breathe by keeping its long, flexible snout just above the surface. The matamata's legs and neck are fringed with little bits of flesh that float gently in the water and draw the attention of a hungry fish, frog, tadpole, or water beetle that swims near the fleshy "bait." The turtle then opens its wide jaws and sucks in a mouthful of water, prey and all.

The matamata's bumpy, algae-covered shell and fringed neck camouflage it from its unsuspecting prey.

Piranha skull

The River Shark

If you saw a list of the world's most dangerous fish, you would likely find the piranha near the top. Of the 2,500 kinds of fish that live in the Amazon River, this fierce creature, also called the "river shark," is the best known. Several kinds of piranhas wander the river, but the red piranha is the most dangerous. About 16 inches long and weighing in at nearly four pounds, this fish is equipped with an arsenal of stabbing, cutting teeth. (In fact, because the teeth slide past each other like scissor blades, natives sometimes use the dried jaws of red piranhas as hair clippers!) Taking about a cubic inch of flesh with each bite, an individual fish can do incredible damage, but the greatest danger lies in the fact that these creatures sometimes travel in groups of hundreds. An animal as large as a cow can be devoured in just a few minutes, leaving nothing but bare bones.

Other fish usually make up the piranhas' diet, but, particularly during the dry season when water levels drop and food is scarce, these ferocious creatures will eat almost anything. Huge schools then gather together. They prowl throughout the river, but they seem to prefer shallow water near wide bends in the river. The scent of blood attracts them, as does the splashing of animals. Local residents avoid swimming in shallow water at these times.

Piranhas do perform a service, although it is a strange one. The ground where certain tribes live is marshy and wet, making it difficult for the people to bury their dead. In such areas, bodies are lowered into the water, where the bones are picked clean by piranhas. The skeletal remains are then decorated and laid to rest in above-ground burial sites.

Carnivorous piranhas, feeding in packs of hundreds, can devour an animal as large as a cow in a few short moments.

Large worker ant

The March of the Ants

One of the most frightful creatures in Central Africa is less than one inch long. Feared by humans and animals alike, it is the driver ant. In a single colony, there may be up to 20 million biting ants, and once they have begun their march, nothing in their path is safe. If the progress of the colony's march threatens human dwellings, fire may be used to repel them, but water is no barrier. At a stream, the ants form bridges by swinging across from overhanging branches, or they gather in a living ball and float to the opposite bank.

Driver ants march in search of food. These ants have no permanent nests. When the queen lays her eggs and the larvae hatch, the search for food is on. The queen and her young move on as well. Animals flee frantically ahead of the advancing horde. The ants move slowly—at no more than 120 feet per hour—but they devour any living thing they overtake, including young birds in nests, frogs, and even larger animals. When the ants rest, they form a shelter called a bivouac (BIV-wak). The bivouac is a living wall of ants. Worker ants build this wall as much as three feet high around the queen and her young. Using grasping leg hooks, a first row of ants clings to a surface. A second row of ants hook onto the first, and in this way the wall is built layer by layer.

As dreadful as driver ants are, in some ways they can be useful to humans. Natives use the stubborn little creatures as a sort of thread or surgical suture. When someone has a cut, a driver ant is coaxed to bite across the wound. Its jaws draw the edges of the skin together. When the jaws are clamped shut, the body of the ant is cut away, leaving the "stitch" in place. Not surprisingly, driver ants are also excellent exterminators. Once the ants have passed through a hut, it is free of insects and rodents for a long period of time.

Once started on their march, driver ants are unstoppable, devouring any living obstacle in their way.

The Freshwater Dolphin

Would you expect to find a dolphin hundreds of miles from a salty ocean? A South American river dolphin called a bouto (BOO-toh) spends its time in fresh water—specifically in the lakes and rivers of the Amazon rain forest. It is a slower swimmer than its sea-going cousins. It generally travels at only about one or two miles an hour—or about as fast as you do when window shopping.

The bouto lives in murky waters, but that doesn't bother the ten-foot-long dolphin. It has special ways to find its meals. One of these is echolocation. As it swims, the dolphin sends out waves of clicking sounds that bounce off objects, and so alert the bouto to possible prey in its path. In this way, the bouto finds the fish it likes to eat. The animal is well suited for this type of search. Its neck is much more flexible than that of most dolphins. In fact, it can turn its head a full 90° to look up or down or from side to side. Because of this flexibility, the bouto can use echolocation to search a very large area in a short time. The bouto also eats shellfish that live on the muddy riverbed. It has special tools to help it locate that sort of prey, too. Lining its snout are stiff sensory bristles, which the dolphin uses to feel its way toward a meal.

This water-dwelling mammal probably doesn't rely very heavily on its tiny eyes when hunting, but it is a curious creature, and it sometimes peeks above the surface of the water to get a look at its surroundings. Native fishermen say that the bouto isn't shy and approaches very close to boats. The animal has little to fear from the fishermen because it is said to be bewitched, and killing one brings very bad luck.

The amazing bouto—a 10-foot-long freshwater dolphin— can rotate its head 90° to search for food.

Typhoons and Monsoons

The word *typhoon* comes from two Chinese words, *ty* and *fung*, that mean "great wind." Actually a tropical cyclone, these windstorms are called typhoons only north of the equator and west of the international date line in the Pacific Ocean. In the Atlantic Ocean, they are called hurricanes. But whatever they're named, these whirling storms are dangerous. A typhoon spawns in tropical waters where the surface temperature is greater than 76°F. Whipping up to wind speeds of 150 miles per hour or more, it moves west toward the Asian continent. Once over land, it can cut a tremendous path of destruction. In 1959, for example, Typhoon Vera struck Japan leaving 4,500 people dead and 40,000 homes smashed to bits. The high winds alone are not responsible for the damage. As a typhoon nears shore, it pushes a huge mound, or surge, of water 15 to 20 feet high ahead of it. When this wave of water washes over the land, it can inflict terrible losses. To prevent such a fate, the Japanese port city of Osaka has spent nearly 600 million dollars to prepare a defense of gates and pumps to hold back or redirect such a surge.

Unlike the stormy winds of a typhoon, monsoon winds blow steadily at certain times of the year. They bring life-giving rains to the forests of India, Africa, southeast Asia, and parts of Australia. *Monsoon* comes from an Arabic word for "season." It is the direction of the monsoon winds (toward the sea from dry land or toward the land from the sea) that determines the dry and wet seasons of the area. The jungles would not survive without the wet season, but monsoon winds can also bring great thunderstorms complete with ear-splitting thunder, flashing bolts of lightning, torrents of pelting rain, and widespread flooding. In 1861, such storms dropped 1,042 inches of rain on Cherrapunji, India. That is the most rain that has fallen in one place in one year anywhere in the world.

To avoid devastation from monsoon rains, people in parts of Indonesia and elsewhere build their homes on stilts.

The Mayans

The Central American rain forests hide a mystery. Buried beneath the tangles of countless roots and vines are the remains of the great Mayan civilization. Where did the Mayan people come from? What was their world like before they were conquered by the Spaniards in the 16th century? The jungle doesn't reveal its secrets easily, but scientists are digging deep among the ruins to find clues to the past. One of the oldest Mayan cities discovered, El Mirador, was built more than 2,000 years ago in what is now the country of Guatemala. Its ruins cover nearly six square miles, or an area large enough to hold 48 amusement parks the size of Disneyland. At one time, thousands of people lived in El Mirador, but for some reason this great city was abandoned and swallowed up by the jungle. Among the limestone buildings uncovered by archaeologists is a pyramid known as El Tigre (EL TEE-gray). At 18 stories high, El Tigre represents just one of the amazing architectural wonders found at El Mirador.

A remarkable people, the ancient Mayans developed a culture that lasted six times longer than that of the Roman Empire. They devised the finest written language in all of the Americas, developed a calendar that is still accurate today, and calculated the orbit of the planet Venus. These people, however, had a very different idea of beauty than we have today. When noble Mayan children were born, their heads were bound between boards. This flattened the sides slightly, giving the Mayans a pin-headed appearance. It was also considered attractive to be cross-eyed. Parents encouraged this condition in their children by tying a ball of wax to a lock of hair that dangled in front of each child's nose.

El Mirador, once a vast Mayan city of many architectural wonders, was abandoned and swallowed up by the jungle.

The Lost City of Angkor

Can you imagine coming face to face with a legend? In 1860, that's just what happened to Henri Mouhot (on-REE moo-OH). He was not searching for a legend in the jungles of Southeast Asia, but for butterflies. Suddenly, he found himself among the huge, vine-draped statues of Angkor Thom (ANG-kor TOM), one of the greatest ancient cities ever built. As far as his eye could see there were towers, buildings, gateways, and roads laced together by banyan trees and strangling figs. There was no sign of humans. Rather, the city was now populated by troops of squealing monkeys, birds, and bats.

According to one legend, Angkor was built by a race of giants. Another legend says the city built itself. In fact, the builders were a powerful people known as the Khmer (k-MAIR). *Angkor Thom,* which means "great city" in the Khmer language, was begun as the capital of the Khmer empire in about 889, in what is now the country of Cambodia. Each ruler added to the jungle metropolis, which once was home to more than a million people. Rice was the main food crop, and the Khmers built a vast irrigation system that made it possible for rice to be grown even in the dry season. Some of the system's canals were as much as 40 miles long. At the edge of the city is *Angkor Wat,* or "great temple." Surrounded by a moat four football fields wide, the temple's outer walls are a mile long on each side and the tallest tower stands 20 stories high.

Why was this magnificent city left to the jungle and forgotten? Perhaps because of war. In 1431, Angkor was conquered and looted by the Thai (TY) people to the north. Soon after, in 1432, a new capital was built at Phnom Penh (p-NAHM PEN), which is still the capital of Cambodia today. Angkor Thom was abandoned to the panther and the cobra and the mists of legend.

If you visited the ancient city of Angkor Thom, you'd find its towers, gateways, and temples completely covered with vines.

The Future of the Rain Forests

Earth's rain forests have stood for millions of years. They are critical to our survival for many reasons. For example, plants absorb carbon dioxide, or CO_2, and in so doing help to control its levels in the air. This is important because CO_2 contributes to the greenhouse effect, which can cause a general warming of the atmosphere. The plants use CO_2 and sunlight to produce their own food, and give off life-giving oxygen in the process.

Now humans are cutting the forests down at a dangerous rate. Trees are felled for timber or are removed for mining or to make room for grazing land. A method of clearing farmland called slash and burn is often used. Trees in an area of forest are cut, dried, and then burned. For two or three years, crops can be grown in the clearing, but the nutrients that had been returned to the soil from the ashes are quickly used up by the crops. When crops can no longer be grown, the land is abandoned. Unprotected, the soil erodes quickly. The hot sun beats down, baking the exposed ground, and topsoil washes away in the rain. Animals begin to disappear as their habitat is destroyed. The forest may reclaim the land, but that takes a very long time, time we cannot afford.

Only about four percent of Earth's rain forests are protected. Saving the forests is not a simple problem. Much of the destruction is taking place in nations with growing populations that depend on the land for survival. One possible solution is to conserve and preserve through better farming, logging, and mining techniques, and through the recycling of forest products. We must also find inexpensive methods of restoring land that has long been left to waste. But solutions must be found, for, in the simple words of a pygmy elder in his faraway jungle home, "When the forest dies, we shall die."

For Further Reading

Causy, Don: *Killer Insects*, New York City, Franklin Watts, 1979.

Coldry, Jennifer: *Discovering Fungi*, New York City, Bookwright Press, 1988.

Forrester, Frank H.: *1001 Questions Answered about the Weather*, New York City, Dover Publications, Inc., 1981.

Harrison, James (ed.): *Nature's Secret World*, New York City, Arco Publishing, 1984.

Hopf, Alice L.: *Bats*, New York City, Dodd, Mead & Co., 1985.

Rowland-Entwistle, Theodore: *Jungles and Rain Forests*, Morristown, New Jersey, Silver Burdett Press, 1987.

Sunden, Ull (ed.): *Remarkable Animals*, Enfield, England, Guiness Superlatives, 1987.

Batten, Mary: *The Tropical Forest*, New York City, Thomas Y. Crowell Co., 1973.

Index